The Definitive Word on Michael Jordan

The Definitive Word on
Michael Jordan

Michael Jordan defines the term "superstar." It's an exaggerated term in the modern era, but he is the model and should be an inspiration for all those playing with and against him. He's in the twilight of his career, but he is still the one to beat.

There has never been a player more special than Michael. He's the complete package, offensively and defensively. He's competitive, and he possesses the ability to raise the level of play for those who play with him. It has never been matched.

I think there is a special respect with Michael and me. I have it for him. And he has it for me. It's a special friendship. He's not a guy you have to talk to every week, or even every month. But he has called upon me for things, and I've called upon him.

Nothing was ever handed to Michael, either. He earned it all. When he first came in you knew he could score and jump, but the Bulls weren't his team and the league wasn't his right away.

Boston and L.A. still had a stranglehold on the league. Then Detroit came along. Detroit was his character builder. The first seven years in the league were tough for Michael. But after that, it's been all his. If you chase something for six or seven years like he did, it makes the winning all the more special.

He came into the league and challenged the standards before him. When he leaves, there will be people who just won't follow the league as passionately as they do now.

New stars will come along, and new fans, but

there will be people who are tied so emotionally to Michael that it won't be the same. New heroes will come along, but there are people who will always want Michael's aura preserved. To them — and there are a lot of them — there will never be another one like Michael Jordan.

Julius Erving was inducted into the Naismith Memorial Basketball Hall of Fame in 1993.

Tim Povtak, who interviewed Dr. J for this story, covers the NBA for the Orlando Sentinel.

"I like the league in Michael Jordan's hands. A lot of people owe him a debt of gratitude."
— Dr. J

I am not going to sit here and lie and say I could see that Michael Jeffrey Jordan was going to be this great when he was in college at North Carolina. Maybe Dean Smith was the only person to see that. But when you look back, it wasn't an accident that Michael was the one who took that shot (a 17-foot jumper that helped propel UNC to a national championship victory over Georgetown) in 1982. The man is phenomenal.

And really, people have run out of words trying to describe him. He was here at Madison Square Garden recently. He scored 44 points. It's not unbelievable that he can score so many points; it's that everybody knows he's shooting and they still can't stop him.

I don't even know why he's going to quit. (Michael said before and during the 1997-98 season that it would likely be his last.) Mike's 35. He's still the best player in the NBA by far. He's at the top of his game. I'm still

"He's Superman. I don't know how he does it — where he gets that energy, his intelligence, his instinct for the game." — former Detroit Pistons head coach Chuck Daly

"If Michael Jordan is not
fearless to his craft, he at
least has we have no solid
evidence that anything is
possible."

— Melissa Isaacson

Chicago Tribune writer

surprised that Chicago did as well as they did without Scottie Pippen. (Pippen missed the Bulls' first 35 games in '97-98 because of foot surgery, but the Bulls went 24-11 in his absence). But, once again, it's a reflection of Michael. I really think the fans of Chicago are spoiled. I don't think until Michael is retired and 10 years down the line will they realize how special and how fortunate they were to have Michael Jordan in a Chicago Bulls uniform. And to a lesser degree, I think you can say that for all the people who watch the NBA. We take the guy for granted. It's amazing the things that he can do on the basketball court. And what really makes Michael so great is that great players elevate their teammates. No player in any sport has elevated the level of his teammates more than what Michael does.

The thing that impresses me the most is Michael's will to win. He just refuses to lose. It's as simple as that. He says, "We're not losing." He impacts his will onto the game. Not too many players can do that in any sport.

Another thing is that Michael is fearless, and he has a big heart, the biggest heart in the league. A lot of times, people have one or the other. They may have the talent, but not the heart. Then some have the heart, but not the talent. Something's missing. But Mike has it all. That's what allows him to stand head and shoulders above his peers.

And let's not forget that he's very smart, too. That's one thing people don't really talk about. Mike has a Ph.D. of the game. He knows the game inside and out. And he knows how to play the game.

When Spike, a.k.a. Mars Blackmon, collaborated with Jordan on a series of Nike commercials, the sky was the limit.

UNSTOPPA-BULL
Entering the 1997-98 season, Air Jordan (a name first used by agent David Falk) had scored 50 or more points 37 times and 60 or more points five times, and his career scoring average of 31.7 points was the highest of any player in NBA/ABA history.

My memories of Michael are many, like those dramatic shots he hit against Cleveland to knock them out of the playoffs. (Jordan's Bulls eliminated the Cavs from the postseason five times from 1987 to 1994.) Most of all, though, I will never forget when he came out of retirement in 1995, and in only his fifth game back, he scored a double-nickel, 55 points, against my Knicks here at the Garden (Lee enjoys $1,000-a-game courtside seats).

When the movie is made about Michael Jeffrey Jordan, he isn't going to be known for scoring all those points, making all those dunks that helped him get the nickname "Air" or for winning all those championships. He's going to be known for just being the best there ever was. That's all.

There's no question in my mind he's the best who ever played this great game. It's always going to be debatable, though. A lot of guys from the older generation will still say Oscar Robertson was the best ever. I talked to (former NBA greats) Clyde Frazier and Earl "The Pearl" Monroe and they still say Oscar. I really didn't see Oscar in his heyday when he played with the Cincinnati Royals. I saw him when he got to Milwaukee and he was on the downside of his career. (Robertson amassed 26,710 points and

Michael surpassed Oscar Robertson for fifth place on the NBA career scoring list with his 26,711th point April 6, 1997, at Orlando.

CHAPTER TWO

9,887 assists during a 14-year NBA career from 1960-61 to 1973-74.)

When the time comes (for Jordan to retire), I just hope the NBA does right by him. They need to preserve his image: those baggy shorts, that bald head, that charming smile, that deadly J. The NBA shouldn't hand him a lame gold watch, a thankful check with a lot of zeroes on it or erect some weak Rocky-like statue in front of the league's Manhattan office as a token of its appreciation.

If the NBA really wanted to immortalize Jordan, it would change its current logo and replace it with Jordan's likeness. The league wouldn't have to hire an artist or look very far for an idea. The high-flying logo — you know, the one with him dunking — on all of his signature sneakers and apparel line would be perfect. Imagine it. Jordan's legacy and image would last forever.

Sure, it would be a monumental move. Unheard of, in fact. But it would be fitting for a player of Jordan's stature. Sure, Magic Johnson and Larry Bird saved the NBA when they arrived in the fall of 1979. And while their accomplishments are many, Jordan stands alone.

It was Jordan — and no one else — who, along with taking his teammates to another level, took this league's play to another standard over the last 10 years. Not only on the court — five championships in seven seasons — but off the court as well.

People who don't even follow the NBA — yes, there are some — know Michael and recognize his talent. All you need to know is that there are only two guys in this world you can call Michael: Jackson and Jordan. That's some company.

The NBA logo, believed to be modeled after legend Jerry West.

Spike Lee thinks the NBA should honor MJ by changing its logo to feature the universally recognized "Jumpman" symbol.

S helton Jackson "Spike" Lee immediately established himself as an innovative and influential filmmaker with his critically acclaimed debut, She's Gotta Have It, in 1986. The movie also spawned the character Mars Blackmon, which he reprised for a series of Nike Air Jordan commercials beginning in 1988.

Lee's other feature credits include Do The Right Thing, Malcolm X, and Clockers. The extremely busy director also has produced several commercials for such companies as Levi's and Ben & Jerry's and

has directed music videos for such artists as Miles Davis and Public Enemy. Still, Lee has found time to feed his sports addiction, filming He Got Game, a movie about a high school basketball phenom (played by Milwaukee Bucks guard and Jordan clothing line pitchman Ray Allen) and taking advantage of Knicks season tickets. (Who could forget his feud with Indiana's Reggie Miller during the 1993-94 playoffs?)

Rob Parker, who interviewed Spike Lee for this story, is a columnist for New York's Newsday.

W hat do I think about Michael Jordan? Simple. He's the greatest player I've ever seen. And I've been around long enough to have seen a lot more than my share, believe me.

But Michael Jordan is something else. It's not only a pleasant job to explain Jordan's brilliance on the basketball court; it's an easy one, basically because he's just so absolutely remarkable.

He's gifted in so many ways, you almost need a calculator to keep track. He is, to me, the most gifted player I've ever seen physically. He has got it all. He's the combination of all the right ingredients: quickness, explosion, speed, athletic ability. He's the one that when I look at basketball players, I'd almost like to say, "Here's my model for the perfect player physically."

But that's not the whole picture, not by a long shot. He also combines two other ingredients.

One is skill. He's as skilled as any player you'd ever want to watch. His shooting has improved throughout his career, and he makes more difficult shots than any player I've ever witnessed. And I think the other ingredient that he brings to the court that probably outweighs any other factor is his competitiveness. He has a will that is second to none.

But if you put all those other elements in there where he has an advantage physically, well, he never gets any questions at all about his competitiveness. He out-competes everyone. I mean, what is there to ask him about his competitiveness? As if you could improve on it. There's just no way.

When I watch him play, the first thing that strikes me is his defense — the way he can stop your best offensive player. And, to me, that's the thing that makes him the greatest player I have ever seen. It's not only the difference he makes

on the offensive end, but also on the defensive end. Think about that. Think about what that means.

Great offensive player and great defensive player.

I've always been a fan of his, even when he was at North Carolina. He didn't really dominate in college, but that's because of the system he played in. But you always could tell he was special. Put it this way: If you watched him play, you knew he was special.

People talk about the difficulties of scouting. But it's not difficult to scout players like him. To me, they stand above the rest by a significant amount. And in watching him play — my goodness — you just had to marvel at the complete package he brought to the game at a very, very young age. He's just unique.

He's like a Magic Johnson in his time. Magic brought a different element to the game because of his size and his ability. This guy (Jordan) dominates the game playing basically without the ball in a way that other players have only been able to dominate in scoring situations.

What sets the truly great players apart is they have a gift. You can't coach it, and you can't teach it. It's a gift. It's the instinct that allows them to be a play ahead. Very few players have that instinct. In his era, a Larry Bird or a Magic Johnson had the gift, but usually those players played a thinking game. Larry Bird and Magic Johnson didn't have Jordan's physical gifts, but they had the intellectual gift to play the game.

Giving Michael Jordan the intellectual gift with the physical gifts almost

San Antonio Spurs center David Robinson once paid almost $6,000 for a signed MJ jersey at a charity auction, outbidding Dallas Stars hockey standout Pat Verbeek.

NEVER AN OFF NIGHT
Jordan scored a career-low eight points on March 22, 1986, at Cleveland before putting together a record-setting string of double-digit performances. He surpassed previous NBA record-holder Kareem Abdul-Jabbar with his 788th consecutive game with 10 or more points on Dec. 30, 1997, against Minnesota.

"Nobody can really play him.
The only way to do it is to
stay with him and keep a
hand in his face. Then you
hope the ball doesn't go in."

— longtime Pistons guard

Joe Dumars

seems unfair. It has been unfair.

I marvel at his mechanics. My impression is that he doesn't dribble the ball just to be dribbling the ball. He gets the ball and he learns how to attack people. To me, the best and most difficult players to guard are not the ones who dribble the ball. It's the ones who step toward you, shoot a jump shot or go by you. He's the most difficult cover for any guard in the league.

And he reads things very quickly. You have to have good eyes to play basketball, and he sees holes differently than other people do. That's a gift. That's a real gift.

It's really interesting to watch Michael work

without the ball. Great players have a nose for the ball, but he's so good messing around without the ball because he changes directions so quickly. In basketball, if you can change directions with and without the ball, you're almost impossible to cover.

With his physical gifts, you can forget it. You're not going to guard him.

A lot of people get such a kick out of his dunk shots, which is only natural, but the number of steals he gets is so important because it sets everything up offensively. So one thing I admire about him is his defensive play, because I know how valuable it is. I've often thought, you

know, they play a kind of conservative defense, but if they played a little bit different kind of defense — maybe pressing and giving him angles to go deflect balls and steal balls — he'd probably lead the league in steals every year. (Jordan led the league in steals three of his first nine seasons.)

People get enamored with dunks and spectacular shots. But if you can just discount that, he's the simplest, purest player who plays the game. He's a beautiful player to watch. There are change of directions, feints, stopping correctly, shooting a jump shot, beautiful form. I mean, to me, he would be pretty if he didn't dunk the ball.

I love the way he plays. If you had the ability to take his dunks away and show kids how to play, this is how you would show them to play the game. It's fundamentals, and his fundamentals are second to none. That's why I think he's incredible. He's been given a gift but he's honed it, worked at it, and he's a pleasure to watch.

To see how effective Jordan is, try to measure what he means to his team, the Chicago Bulls. He's their security blanket. When that security blanket isn't out there, they don't look like the same team. They try to be, but they're not.

Confidence is an incredible thing. When you put a great player on your team, you see that confidence level rise so high. And if you get players who complement him in a system that works for that talent, you have something really special.

Upper Deck included an exclusive interview with Jordan on CD as part of its "23 Nights: The Jordan Experience" card set in 1996. Michael reflected on many of his spectacular performances, including his 63-point barrage against Boston in the 1986 playoffs and his game-winning jumper against Cleveland in the '89 postseason.

Jerry West has directed the basketball operations of the Los Angeles Lakers since 1982 and is regarded as one of the most astute judges of talent in the NBA. Chosen as the NBA's Executive of the Year in 1995, he has been with the Lakers since 1960. A 6-3 shooting guard who played 14 years with the Lakers, he was a 13-time All-Star. West also led the team in regular season scoring seven times, earning the nickname "Mr. Clutch" for his late-game heroics.

When he retired after the 1973-74 season, West was just the third player in league history to pass 25,000 points. His career scoring average of 27 points per game still ranks as the fourth best in the NBA, and his average of 29.1 points-per-game in postseason play is second only to Jordan.

Elected to the NBA Hall of Fame in 1979, West has been associated with the Lakers for all six of their NBA championships.

His respect for Jordan is reciprocated. In the Bulls' annual media guide, Michael lists West as the one player in NBA history he would like to compete against one-on-one.

Thomas Bonk, who interviewed Jerry West for this story, is a writer for the Los Angeles Times.

"Michael has become

much more tolerant

of people and their

limitations."

—Phil Jackson

Whén Michael Jordan entered the NBA, he was thrust into a position that wasn't conducive to a leadership role. Remember, he hadn't played out his full college career at the University of North Carolina. He knew he was ready to turn pro, and he wasn't discouraged to do so. His coaches gave him their blessings to leave. He entered the league as a 21-year-old kid, and he was at the end of the line in terms of seniority.

Michael soon discovered that there wasn't much leadership around the league, and there certainly wasn't much to be found with his new Bulls team. Immediately, Michael saw that his talent level was above and beyond that of many of the players around him. His leadership role was to challenge opponents and be competitive on the court, and in that regard, Michael was terrific. He single-handedly took over ball games, put his team on his back and influenced games with his remarkable feats. He didn't lead by example as much as he did by sheer athletic effort. Soon everybody got enthused about this guy.

That's why the Bulls have the following that they do today. His spectacular performances and desire to win helped build a core of fans that grew into what it is today. In itself, that was leadership — not overt, mind you,

MICHAEL AND THE JORDANAIRS
Jordan's role as franchise cornerstone was understood almost from the beginning. After Jerry Reinsdorf purchased the Bulls in 1985, he challenged Jerry Krause, new vice president of basketball operations, to find players who would complement MJ. Chicago soon traded for forward Charles Oakley and signed free agent guard John Paxson.

"We're the leaders of this team together, but he's in control all the time. He's there whenever anyone needs him."

— Bulls teammate Scottie Pippen

he had been demoted from captain to co-captain. He respected Bill even though he knew that he was physically limited.

At that point, Michael was able to lead from a position of adaptation. He allowed people to enter his realm. They could score points. They could share the glory. He gave praise to his teammates. At the same time, he could be awfully hard on them. He could become extremely angry, even thrash the team on occasion, which in some respects isn't all bad.

A defining moment in Michael's development as team leader occurred in Miami in 1990, immediately following the All-Star Game, which several of our players either played in or attended. After we resumed our season with a victory there, we played at Orlando the next evening. We had a big lead before the guys ran out of gas and finally lost in overtime (135-129). I was extremely angry, but it was Michael who made his teammates understand that it was time to step up and play to a responsible level. He was able to back my sentiment that, hey, there was a time to have fun and to enjoy this world, but there was also a time to turn things away and be responsible about what you had to do. (The Bulls responded by going on a 9-0 tear and returned to the Eastern Conference finals.)

Michael didn't attain the legendary status of a Bird or Magic until his Bulls became champions —— and graced the box of the "Cereal of Champions."

In the time since he has returned to the game, Michael has become much more tolerant of people and their limitations in the game in light of the fact that they try hard. He understands that everyone isn't equally gifted, and that effort doesn't always get the job done. Michael is much more able to pat somebody on the behind and say, "Don't worry about it." He also has become more vocal in his leadership role. A teammate might ask him, "Well, what do you think, Michael?" Now he's able to communicate his answer in a more concise manner than he did earlier in his career.

For instance, in our final two playoff series in 1995-96, teams were getting physical with Steve Kerr and he was missing shots. I told Michael, "Give him a little bit of encouragement." And he said, "Yeah, I was meaning to do that." Michael was able to do something that wasn't easy for him to do in the past, and that was help a guy who was struggling.

Michael lifted Steve Kerr's spirits after the fellow guard missed a crucial three-point attempt in Game 4 of the '97 Finals against Utah. Jordan then dished the ball to Kerr for the game- and series-winning jumper in Game 6 as the Bulls wrapped up their fifth title in seven years.

*P*hil Jackson is one of only nine men to be part of an NBA championship team as both a coach and a player, but it has been as the Bulls' head coach that Jackson has truly left his mark on the game. The all-time winningest coach in franchise history reached the 200-victory plateau in 270 games, fastest of any head man in NBA history. The Bulls won five championships in seven years under Jackson from 1991 to '97. Their combined 141 regular season victories in 1995-96 and 1996-97 completed a two-year lesson in domination, the likes of which the NBA had never seen.

Paul Ladewski, who interviewed Phil Jackson for this story, covers the NBA and Bulls for the Daily Southtown Economist.

time, if you are the biggest kid, they stick you under the basket and they don't want you to handle the ball.

They want the other kids to handle it. But it's kind of nice when you grow up like him and are not the biggest kid, and you get to do all those things like learning how to handle the ball and developing some offensive moves. The kid who took the final varsity spot (Leroy Smith) was also a sophomore but was 6-5 or 6-6 then. He didn't have the skills that Mike had, and part of the reason was he ended up playing center all that time.

Mike was the best we had, even as a junior. He always had good basketball skills. He always played guard because he was smaller. As he grew, (his skills and experience) just made it a whole lot easier for him.

Everybody respected his game because he always played hard. He was always a competitor, and that is what they admired more than anything else. He played pretty much the way he does now — he plays to win.

When he was a junior, the attention was mostly local. He didn't start getting a lot of national attention until the summer between his junior and senior season when he went to the camps. He was always confident; it didn't take camp for him to realize he could play.

Enviromint marketed an MJ coin, which was licensed through Upper Deck Authenticated after the Bulls' third title of the '90s.

"Michael was one of the best-kept secrets in the country. He worked harder than anybody, even though he had enough talent that he probably didn't have to."

—Ron Coley, Laney coach

Even when he went into the NBA, he was not a great shooter. He's an even better shooter late in his career than when he first got there.

Part of that is having to adjust your game as you get older. You can't just run by everybody and jump over them. He shot the ball well in high school. A lot of kids are good shooters in high school, because they are bigger than other kids and they don't have someone in their face. He was never a bad shooter, but the difference is that as he moved up (from high school to college to the pros) he learned to get his shot off a whole lot quicker and improved his range.

When he went to the pros, he didn't have three-point range. He hit some threes, but he showed a lot of leadership ability, even in high

wasn't a real threat like later on. You back off him now, he'll hit the shot.

Michael has never thought he was as good as he could be. Even now. I don't think he's ever had the attitude that, "I don't need to work." One thing he has always done is work extremely hard, whether it's at practices, in games or in the off-season. I think that is what has separated him from others who have a lot of talent.

He just didn't like to lose. When we lost in the state playoffs his senior year, he was upset, particularly because we lost to a county rival. He's always been competitive. That hasn't changed, and I guess that never will. So he

school. The nice part is to look back and know where he was versus where he is now. He has improved his game so much . . . so much.

The kids who come in now, they know he played here and they see what he has done in the pros. But as far as the things that he did to get there, we talk about it to our players. We don't necessarily talk about what he does on the court, but his work ethic. "You are never going to be able to do the things he does, but you can have the work ethic that he has."

If they do that, then we have no complaints. People talk about role models, but how many people are going to grow to be 6-6 and have his hands and his abilities? It's rare. The other things that he did, the way he approached the game, is what they need to try and have.

It's kind of a storybook life for him in a lot of ways. He's worked hard to get where he is. He's been in the right place at the right time. He hit the shot to win the NCAA championship his freshman year (as North Carolina upended Georgetown, 63-62). A lot of it had to do with

> "I had no idea he was that good of a player until I had him for the Olympics. The kid is a superior athlete — the best I've ever seen."
> — Bobby Knight, coach of the gold medal 1984 U.S. Olympic team, of which Jordan was co-captain.

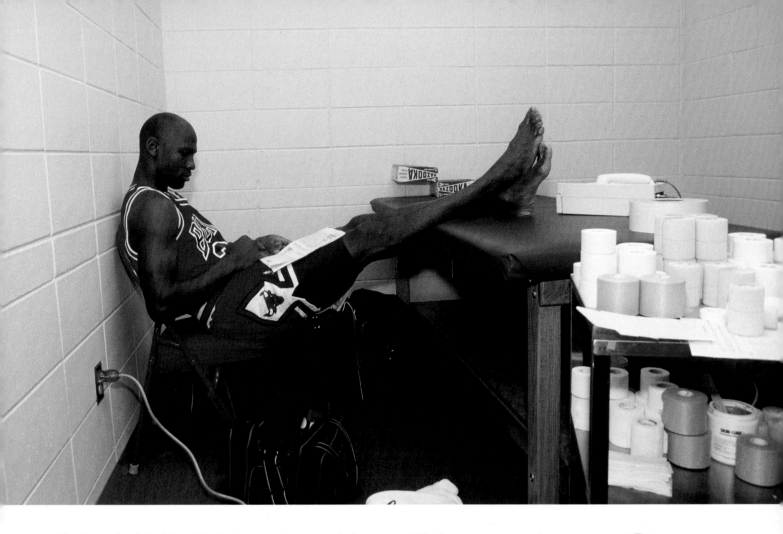

him doing the right things. You don't ever antic-ipate getting another player like him. You hope to, but they don't come often. As a coach, you hope you did some things right. It's hard to take any credit for somebody who gets to where he is. But you just hope you did some things right and made a difference. You just look back at him and shake your head a little bit. He is a once-in-a-lifetime kind of player.

F red Lynch is the athletic director at Laney High School and has been the head boys basketball coach since 1983, posting a 223-133 record in his first 14 seasons. He was Jordan's ninth-grade coach, then was an assistant on the Laney varsity squad paced by Jordan in 1979-80 and 1980-81.

Jordan averaged 27 points per game as a senior at Laney, where he earned prep All-America honors.

His nickname was "Magic Mike," as evidenced by the picture he sent of himself to the Raleigh News & Observer *for its All-East team his senior year. Jordan posed on the hood of his car for the picture, basketball in hand and "Magic Mike" personalized license plate in full view.*

There's no wizardry, however, to MJ's rapid ascent from JV standout to highly regarded recruit: he grew from about 6-feet to about 6-4 between his sophomore and junior seasons. With the added height, and Lynch's coaching, Jordan's game went to another level.

Bill Woodward, who interviewed Fred Lynch for this story, covers high school sports for the Raleigh News & Observer.

Michael's relationship with Nike began in 1984 and by '97 it had evolved into the Jordan brand, placing the Jumpman logo on socks and other apparel.

After believing we should have won the national championship the year previously, Michael Jordan came in and gave us another guy in 1981-82. At the time, we didn't know how great he would be or how much of an impact he would have, but we felt with James Worthy and the supporting cast, we had a crew. We just wanted to go play.

Everybody picked us to be No. 1. It's not like we had to live by it. We didn't really pay attention to it, but we had talent on that team. Michael was good, but not like he is today. Still, he made an impact, especially when we played within our league. That's when he started branching out more and more, showing the dunks and the moves.

He caught on quickly. He was a freshman, and even though freshmen weren't supposed to really play, this man out of Wilmington had to play. He did some things that freshmen are not supposed to do. Sometimes he would take over games. (Jordan became the Atlantic Coast Conference Rookie of the Year and hit the game-winning basket — known simply as "The Shot" — in a dramatic 63-62 victory over Georgetown for the national championship.)

Still, Michael fit well in head coach Dean Smith's system. He had talent beyond that of a freshman. Freshmen normally are supposed to learn and grow into their sophomore years. With the skills he came in with, he

A SMOOTH TRANSITION
Jordan was a perfect fit in 1982 for an already multifaceted North Carolina lineup. The skinny, young guard from Wilmington joined starters Sam Perkins, James Worthy, Jimmy Black and Matt Doherty as the Tar Heels cruised to their first NCAA title under Dean Smith.

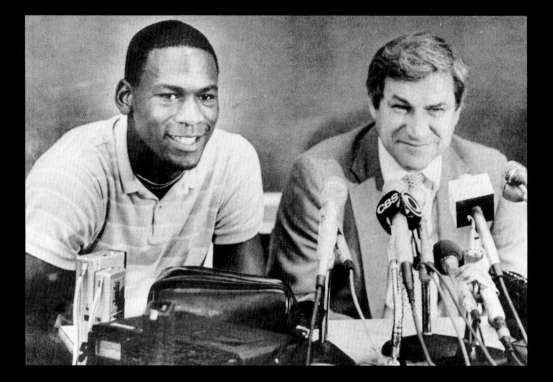

Now you get groomed as soon as you get out of high school. I think when people saw The Shot (a 17-footer with 17 seconds remaining at the Superdome in New Orleans), as big as that was for him as a freshman, it paved the way for other freshmen to have more responsibility to the game.

He handled it well. He became the North Carolina favorite. You had a guy who was from North Carolina, who went to North Carolina, and now you had someone to associate with North Carolina.

When the bells rang around him from that shot, it gave him a sense of responsibility. The next year he was a veteran as a sophomore. With the talent that he had, he was able to do that.

Coach Smith prepared Michael mentally to keep his ego in check. Michael always talked about other people on the team. He handled it and carried the responsibility well. But when it came to the game, he was all-out, just like anybody else.

When you go to a program like that, it gives you more of a sense of confidence. When you see you can win together and play unselfishly, the program really dictates your progress and reputation from thereon. North Carolina was always a school where we had winning ways. When you have that, you go a little further. That helped propel me into the NBA. So having that respect for the game, and not thinking you are bigger than the game, really helps you.

People talk about Coach holding Michael down. We had so much talent, you didn't have to score 30 points per game. Everybody played together, and Michael respected that. He didn't have to do all the work all night long. College wasn't like that.

That's why we went so far. We played unselfishly, and we liked each other. If you scored within the system, you scored. But if you had a good night, you made sure you complimented the guys who got you the ball. That was everybody's mentality.

The togetherness has continued. There is a Carolina kind of closeness within the NBA, and we get to see everybody who is in the pros. Michael's fame makes it different for him. I can only see Michael on the court. He's still levelheaded, but with the fame that he has, he's all over. You can't go out with him. He can't walk the malls like an ordinary person such as myself. It's almost a challenge for him to sneak out. So it's kind of hard to see him, but I do say, "hello."

I've been around two people with the persona that he exudes: Magic Johnson and James

"That shot gave me more confidence to improve as a player than any other situation. It's frightening to think of how things would have been if I had missed."

— Jordan

Worthy. Michael has the personality to fit everybody's mindset of being a total player on and off the court. He's genuine to the fact of what he has, and he respects it. He's not like a Wilt Chamberlain, who brags about it. The way Coach trained us in college, that is the mentality Michael has now — make sure you give

thanks to the people who got you there. I think that is the mentality we all have. Even though he is on a bigger scale, he is still thankful for what he has.

We all have almost the same sentiments for Coach. When he retired (before the 1997-98 season with 879 victories, the most by a NCAA

S am Perkins is one of many basketball players from New York to attend North Carolina. He also happens to be one of the most beloved Tar Heels. His smooth playing style and polite, soft-spoken manner made him a fan favorite from the beginning.

Perkins, the 1980-81 ACC Rookie of the Year and MVP of the ACC tournament, is still the school's career leader in rebounds with 1,167. In addition to being teammates at North Carolina, Perkins and Jordan played on the gold medal winning 1984 U.S. Olympic team coached by Bob Knight.

They were both first-team All-Americans in '84, and Perkins and Jordan entered the NBA draft together following the season when Jordan decided to leave school a year early.

Perkins played six seasons with the Dallas Mavericks before signing with the Los Angeles Lakers in 1990. He and former UNC teammate James Worthy competed against Jordan's Chicago Bulls in the 1991 NBA Finals.

Perkins joined the Seattle SuperSonics and head coach George Karl, also a former Tar Heel, during the 1992-93 season.

> Referred to as "The Shot" or "The Shot, Part II" is Jordan's buzzer-beating jumper over Cleveland's Craig Ehlo in the fifth and final game of the Bulls' 1989 playoff series with the Cavs.

Division I basketball coach), we almost all said the same things, but we never rehearsed them or talked about them. The way he taught us how to play and respect one another stayed with us, especially for me. I'm sure it is the same way for Michael, James Worthy, Jimmy Black, Brad Daugherty . . . it goes down the line.

Perkins, who earned a degree in communications, started a production company in Seattle to produce music for sporting events. He also is the host of a local radio show.

Eddy Landreth, who interviewed Sam Perkins for this story, is a freelance writer based in Chapel Hill, N.C.

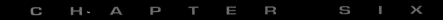

would see that the

were going to be

Kevin Loughery

Going into the 1984 draft there was no doubt that Jordan would be available. The situation was that Hakeem Olajuwon was going to be No. 1 and Sam Bowie was the No. 2 choice.

Everybody since has criticized Portland for the decision to take Bowie second, and certainly, in retrospect, after Bowie had so many physical problems (playing just 139 games in five seasons with the Trail Blazers), you've heard more and more about it. But they had All-Star guard Clyde Drexler and it was a case where Drexler was going to be there for them.

So it was a year when Michael was going to fall because of the teams ahead of us and the needs they had.

Once we got to camp with Michael, first of all, we realized he was a better shooter than some other people thought. We knew of his athletic skills, but North Carolina was mostly a passing team. So his game was ready, which you knew, because he was exposed to Dean Smith.

But even early, there were several hints that he was able to handle the ball and had that all-around game. And we knew we could take advantage of that.

First of all, we weren't very talented. We had some role players outside of Michael and we had some very young players. So we decided with Michael, once we saw how good he was, that we would use him as much as we could. (Jordan took the reins of a lackluster offense and scored an aver-

BLUE—BLOODED
Jordan traded his Carolina colors for Chicago's red and black in 1984 . . . sort of. He continued to wear his Tar Heels shorts under his Bulls uniform for good luck.

"Fans wanted to rip his jer-

sey right off him. He wasn't

a basketball player, he was

a rock star."

— Bulls teammate

Orlando Woolridge

the game, even though he only was a rookie and only had three years in the college game.

What people fail to realize about Michael is that he's strong in his knowledge of the game, real strong. He came out of college tremendously coached, and that's an advantage, too. And he didn't have a whole lot of adjustment.

He pushed from Day One. No matter what the other players did, he pushed them. His teammates could see that he was going to be a big-time player. And he just has natural leadership, which you can't teach.

There's no doubt, when we were playing, he always wanted every shot at the end. You could tell by his attitude and his expression.

I was watching a game the other night with my son when the Bulls were playing someone and were down to the last shot. As I was watching, I said to my son, "The shot's not for Michael." And sure enough, Toni Kukoc took it. You could just see it in Michael's face when he was coming out of the huddle.

And that's the way it's always been. No matter what the situation, when he had the last shot, Michael wanted the ball.

I coached Julius Erving when he was young, but not quite as young. I think the difference I've seen is that Michael had unbelievable

Bulls head coach Kevin Loughery didn't bother with slowly bringing along his star rookie — and that was just fine with Michael. Jordan took the Bulls by the horns, scoring 37 points in just his third game as Chicago beat Milwaukee, 116-110.

confidence in himself and was comfortable being more of one of the actual leaders. Doc, on the other hand, was the easiest star you could coach. But Michael's leadership was incredible, even to the point where if some of his teammates weren't happy with Michael, it's because Michael would push them too hard. Michael just wanted to win.

He wanted to win in every situation, even in practice. Because of that, we used to switch teams, like when we were playing to 10. He'd get his team up 7-0, and then I'd put him on the other team. That would really tick him off.

I think there are very few players who had what Michael had. There's Magic Johnson, and there's Larry Bird. But there are so few.

Yet when you look back to when Michael first arrived, I don't think you could have possibly envisioned that he would have had this impact, because he's not a center, not a big man. But, as Michael has shown, there are a lot of other things involved in reaching a championship level of play.

If you were to ask me now whether it would have been easier to coach him at this stage of his career or coach him then, I think it would be easier now. It's much easier to win. (The Bulls went 38-44 during Jordan's rookie campaign in

In Rookie of the Year balloting Jordan beat out his nearest competitor, No. 1 draft pick Hakeem Olajuwon (battling MJ), by 20 votes. Sam Bowie (above), the second pick, made the All-Rookie Team but suffered from leg and foot problems the remainder of his career.

'84-85 and 69-13 in '96-97.) I don't care what people say.

People talk about how there's such great pressure to win a championship. Well, the pressure's on the guy who's losing. You have to win. The pressure to win on a losing team starts at the beginning of the season. The pressure to win with great teams starts in April.

Since I coached Michael, I've played golf with him and I've seen him often. I don't spend a lot of time with Michael, but I think he's the type of person who, if he spotted me walking into a restaurant, he'd sit down and talk. We still usually play golf once a year.

The Michael you see today, because he's done such a great job in the corporate world for himself, you'd think he's different than he is. But he's not like that.

To me, there are five people who belong on the same court with Michael, people who have shaped the game. There's Doc, Magic, Bird and the commissioner (David Stern). Those are the ones we owe an awful lot to.

But Michael's had the biggest impact.

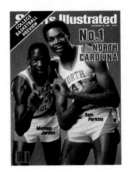

Young Michael made his first appearance on the cover of *Sports Illustrated* with teammate and buddy Sam Perkins in 1983. Since then, *SI* has featured Jordan as its cover subject more than 40 times — a record for an athlete in any sport.

By the time Chicago Bulls head coach Kevin Loughery received a talented rookie guard out of North Carolina with the No. 3 pick in the 1984 draft, Loughery already had established his own legend in coaching circles.

Loughery, in fact, still can be found in the NBA record book, although his mark isn't one he's particularly proud of. He wound up coaching the 1972-73 Philadelphia 76ers to a 5-26 finish after stepping in for dismissed mentor Roy Rubin. That team closed with an all-time NBA-worst 9-73 record.

But the brief stint as player-coach launched a sideline career that saw the former Baltimore Bullets guard coach the New York Nets to ABA championships in two of the next three seasons.

From there, Loughery continued his coaching career in the NBA with New Jersey, Atlanta and then Chicago, where he was rewarded with the drafting of Jordan after his first season. With Jordan aboard, Loughery's Bulls improved 11 games, going from 27-55 in 1983-84 to 38-44.

Alas, MJ's rookie season was Loughery's last in Chicago, with a new front office showing Loughery the door. From there, Loughery coached Washington and Miami before moving into the Heat's front office in 1995. These days, Loughery keeps tabs on Jordan and many of his other former players by viewing games on his satellite dish at his Atlanta home and working late-season and playoff games for ESPN Radio.

Ira Winderman, who interviewed Kevin Loughery for this story, covers professional basketball for the Sun-Sentinel of South Florida.

CHAPTER SEVEN

THE COMPETITOR

"He wants to win. And he usually wants to lick you [bad]."

— Charles Barkley

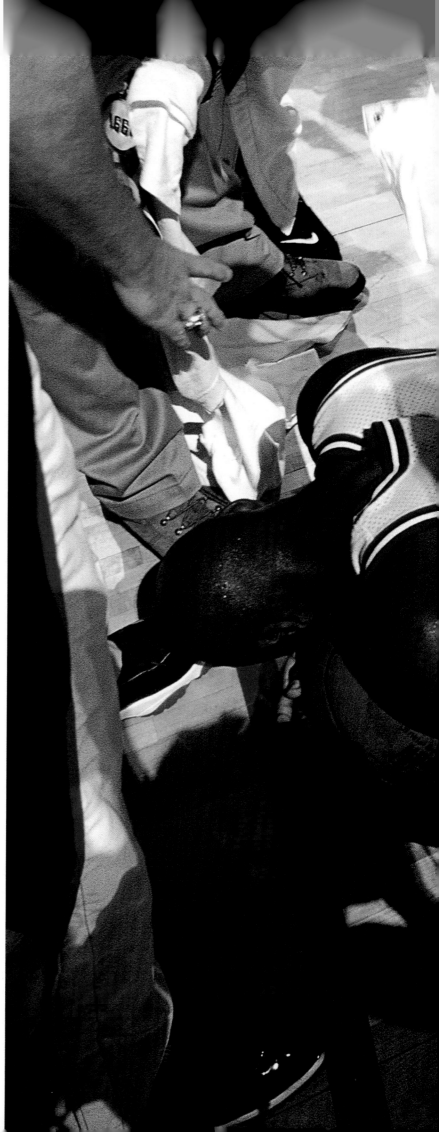

The first time I met Michael Jordan was at the 1984 Olympic Trials. The thing is he wasn't the Michael Jordan you think of today. He hadn't won all those titles yet. He was still a college kid, but you could see that competitive nature. He wanted to win, even in practice. I've always been competitive. That's something that was in me even in high school. And I could recognize that in Michael.

It comes out anytime you compete with Michael — golf, cards, basketball, whatever. It doesn't matter. He wants to win. And he usually wants to kick your (butt). You notice how competitive he is because he wants to win at everything. And I mean everything. When we play golf together, he's very competitive. When we play cards together, he's very competitive.

I think you have to have that competitive nature. That's something I've never lost, and I don't think I could ever lose it. Michael's the

"Winning a championship, even for the stars, is like a stamp of approval. It gives them a feeling that, 'Now I've done it.'" — Doug Collins, Bulls head coach from 1986-89

same way. What do you think it is that allows him to have success like he has, where he wins championship after championship? You absolutely need that in this game if you want to stay on top.

Magic Johnson had it, Larry Bird had it, and Michael has it, too. That's what drives Michael. To win a couple of championships, you have to have that killer instinct and competitive nature. And Michael has five (titles). Like I said, Magic and Larry Bird had it, but Michael might take it to a whole other level.

I think the one thing that brought me and Michael together was how competitive we were. You would think that would make us rivals, but it didn't. I think the same thing happened to Magic and Larry Bird. I think they became friends because they wanted to win so bad. It's the same with me and Michael.

Michael wants to win every game. Los Angeles Lakers head coach Del Harris said something very interesting to me once (after a 113-103 double-overtime win by the Lakers on

A 1997 Upper Deck Jordan boxed set featured a golf ball with Jordan's facsimile signature.

Nov. 14, 1997, at Houston). He said, "You won this game for my team in overtime." I said, "What do you mean?" He said, "You were trying to will your team to win. We picked up on that and used it."

I know that in my prime, I could say to myself, "We are not going to lose this game." I tried to do that against the Lakers. I was thinking, "There's only one ball, so if I get all the rebounds, we're going to win the game." In my prime, I could do that. The difference is that Michael keeps doing that. He has done that throughout his career. You sit there at home and you're thinking, "Damn, Michael is not going to let his team lose the game." And that's when you see it. Suddenly the Bulls put on a run. I see that probably 50 times a year.

That competitiveness has driven him to excel in every aspect of the game. But he's not just a great offensive player. A lot of guys can score, maybe not like Michael, but they can score. But Michael wants to be able to beat you in other ways, too. He can take over a game with his defense, and I've seen him do it. He can even rebound when he thinks he has to.

Why (strive to excel like that)? Because he wants to compete on any level he chooses. How many other players can do that? None, that's how many. He's probably the most complete player ever. What else can you say? He's definitely the most complete player ever.

I think anytime a young player plays against an established player, the young player wants to come at him. They want to see if the established player still has it. And Michael goes through that every night. But I think that once you have become established, you want to stay on the mountain top. That's how Michael keeps his edge. It's good being on top. It's very good. And Michael's been on top for a long time now.

I think (the spirit of competition) is one thing that has helped us. More than anything else, I think that's the thing that started it off. He's always been supportive of me. When I was in Philadelphia, he would always tell me not to get frustrated, that I wasn't the reason we were losing. He would always come up to me after games in Philly and say that I wasn't the problem. Just talking to him was helpful.

I'm good friends with Karl Malone, Patrick Ewing and David Robinson, but I want to kill them when I play. Even growing up as a little kid, the person you want to beat more than anybody is your brother or your best friend. When I play against Michael, I try to kill him because

"Michael somehow or another finds a way to rejuvenate himself. At this age, that surprised us." — Bulls head coach Phil Jackson in 1997

he's going to try and kill me. I know how he is.

Our personalities just clicked. He hates losing, so we're a lot alike. (The difference between reality and) the public perception of us is like night and day. He loves to have fun and so do I. Hey, I look at him as a brother.

C harles Barkley, an avid golfer and the best basketball player to ever come out of Leeds, Ala., has been a friend of Michael Jordan for more than a decade. The duo took their rivalry into the national spotlight in the 1993 NBA Finals, when Barkley's Suns lost to the Bulls in six games.

Sir Charles performed admirably in that series, averaging 27.3 points per game to go along with 13 rebounds and five assists. But indicative of the rivalry between the two, Jordan would not be overshadowed, setting a Finals record with his 41 points per game average in leading the Bulls to their third straight title.

Before the 1996-97 season, Barkley was traded to the Houston Rockets, where he teamed with Clyde Drexler and Hakeem Olajuwon to form one of the league's more formidable (and oldest) trio of stars.

Just as Barkley has fond memories of his first meeting with Jordan, Michael also remembers his first impressions of Charles.

"When I first met him, he thought he could guard me as much as I could guard him," Jordan said with a laugh. "We were both embarrassed in those scenarios."

Michael Murphy, who interviewed Charles Barkley for this story, covers the Rockets for the Houston Chronicle.

W hen you look at Michael Jordan as the businessman, you see someone who has cultivated relationships with companies over a long period of time. He has met with their chairmen and has golfed with them, socialized with them and has spent time with them. And he has learned a lot.

He is not just one of those guys who has always said, "Well, I'm going to do this endorsement, make some money and move on to the next one." (Jordan signed a $2.5 million deal with Nike in '84, helping build the shoe and apparel company into a $9-billion-a-year juggernaut that in 1998 was responsible for covering the feet of about 260 NBA players.)

I think you could put Michael in the same class of businessmen as he is

PITCHMAN
Jordan has served as a spokesman for a long list of companies, including McDonald's, Coca-Cola, Bijan (Michael Jordan cologne), Oakley, WorldCom, Sara Lee (Ballpark Franks, Hanes), CBS Sportsline, Upper Deck, General Mills (Wheaties), AMF and Rayovac.

"Nike has done such a job of promoting me that I've turned into a dream. To a lot of people, I'm just a person who stars in commercials."

— Jordan

a basketball player. He's the chief executive officer, chairman of the board and vice chairman as a player. But he is more as a businessman. Some players have the business acumen. I think Michael, from his rookie season to 1998, probably has grown and matured and become more sophisticated than any player in the game.

A lot of it has to do with seeing the big picture. He has great representation, and his greatness has allowed him to have doors opened that otherwise would not have been opened. But he's taken great advantage of that.

I think he's probably learned a lot along the way by himself, because he knows that when this is all over he's going to have an incredible position in his own company that he has started, and he'll have to be able to run that. So he is smart enough and has learned enough to be able to one day cross over and be very successful.

He's in board meetings; he sees how business leaders interact. And I'm sure he watches how they act and sees what they say. Some people see an air of success. He models it. He's very intuitive and he watches.

I think players can handle doing things dur-

> "You must make a superstar like Michael scarce enough to be interesting, yet available enough to be popular. It is a constant balancing act . . . "
> — MJ's agent, David Falk

ing the season, these outside business interests, if, in fact, they organize their schedule. His schedule is so organized, in the fact that he probably does everything. I mean, they can do a commercial on an off day, and players can do it, if it's organized.

The difference is he's the one who dictates how long it's going to take. He's one of these guys who is a one-take guy. He doesn't have to spend a thousand takes. He can come in and do it three or four times, because he's so good at it, and it's done and over with.

I think there's a real organizational benefit on his side, where he is able to do these things where it doesn't affect his head and he can still perform. (A commercial titled "CEO Jordan" makes light of this strength as Michael slips into a business suit at halftime of a game, sprints to the office to handle a plethora of business duties, then returns to the United Center and completes a 40-point outing in his wing tips.) A lot of guys can't do it.

Because of who he is and how he handles himself, you, as a coach, are not bothered by having your players wear his sneakers. It's a business side of it. I don't think it affects the players when they're playing.

And if, in fact, Michael ever picked one of the Miami Heat players to wear his line of

> Heat head coach Pat Riley says he sees nothing wrong with his players emulating Jordan the business-man — as long as it doesn't affect their on-court perfor-mance.

talk. And there's nothing wrong with that.

I do believe coaches who are out in front of their organizations are role models in the business community. So a coat and tie and being well-groomed is part of the whole thing. It isn't an act. I don't do it because I want to be on *GQ*. I do it because I think that's what should be done. I think Michael is the same way.

Michael is someone I've followed. I've read his books. He is a very interesting personality, because he knows how to do it — how to get it done — whatever it is. Get the game done, get the performance done, get the corporate world done.

But I do think he is one who is so protective of his time, so very protective of it, that he still does find time for his family in addition to everything else he has to do.

I have read him and I have witnessed him change his dialogue and how he talks and what he says. And he does have a great depth to him and a great substance to him. I think a lot of it is something that came from within, and some of it is learned. Like with me, I've learned a lot from other people, and I use it.

He is someone who has stayed above it all (from losing teams early in his career to gambling allegations to the untimely death of his

Jordan says he hopes his golf company, owned by AMF, will "inspire more people to play the game." If not, perhaps visitors of the company's retail stores will feel the urge to purchase Michael memorabilia.

father to career switches). He has kept his name above it.

Known for his team-building in both the corporate and athletic worlds, Pat Riley is one of the nation's highest-paid corporate speakers as well as one of the highest-paid coaches in the NBA.

Since his NBA championship days with the Los Angeles Lakers (his teams won titles in 1982, '85, '87, '88), Riley has reshaped the futures of both the New York Knicks and Miami Heat. Ironically, in both cases, Riley's greatest roadblock to championships has been Michael Jordan.

The respect Jordan has cultivated in the basketball world is one that Riley has taken pause to appreciate. "I do believe that players bow down and revere him so much that they don't compete against him," Riley says. While a clear rivalry is in place between the two, there also is a healthy respect. Like Riley, Jordan has found significant success in the business world.

Riley's motivational tome, The Winner Within, was a best-seller among corporate strategists interested in emulating his success in the basketball realm.

Ira Winderman, who interviewed Pat Riley for this story, covers the NBA for the Sun-Sentinel of South Florida.

Patrons of Michael Jordan's, The Restaurant may stuff this shopping bag full of items from the souvenir shop. Typical items emblazoned with the Chicago restaurant logo are for sale as well as select Nike gear and Chicago Bulls merchandise. Diners may feast on American cuisine in the sports bar or one of the two dining rooms.

> "Talent is never enough. With few exceptions the best players are the hardest workers."
>
> — Magic Johnson

Michael Jordan's lasting imprint on basketball is something I could easily write an entire book about. He's probably the one player who has made the biggest impact in terms of . . . well . . . just everything. He's the player who's won, the player who's made the most money off the court, the player who's affected so many generations.

He will always have an impact, even when he's done. He's one of those players who lives on. Just remember this: He's the most celebrated athlete out there. Forget basketball player. This guy is just a superstar no matter where he is, on the court or off. And nobody has done that.

On the court, I look at the way he was and the way he is now. Michael looked at what was going on with Larry Bird and myself and he

"People who are pressing to know what life is going to be like without him wearing No. 23 are the same kind of people who want to know how Penn & Teller do their tricks. Let's all just enjoy the magic." — Dick Ebersol, president, NBC Sports

You know, dominating the game from the backcourt is another thing to think about. First of all, it's harder to dominate in the backcourt because you've got to do so many more things. You've got to bring it up, you've got to get everybody in their position, you've got to understand when you have to take over.

So, see, there are a lot of mental things going on from the backcourt. Michael has been head and shoulders above the rest in getting this part done. That's what makes him so much more special, dominating from his position. Michael looks up and he knows those other four guys are all looking at him, and he still dominates. It's like he's saying, "I'm going to go by you and go by you. Then, when I get to you, I'm going to go around you. And then, the last guy, I'm going to dunk on you!"

He's got the inside game, outside game and he can drive around you. So he's unstoppable. But people didn't give him credit for all those things. Then again, he never really has gotten credit for his defense either, because he can shut you down. He's got the best anticipation in the game. He understands how to play passing lanes.

Jordan said he was with his family when he missed a "mandatory" trip to the White House after the Bulls' first title in '91. But MJ has been a regular in D.C. since then — and there's still no doubting his feelings for wife Juanita and the kids.

I know what he has meant to the game. You don't measure it in dollars, even though Michael has made plenty of those. And the only reason Kevin Garnett can get $128 million (the forward signed a six-year, $128-million deal with the Timberwolves in '97) is because of three guys: me, Larry and Michael. And of the three, two of us are retired. But Michael is still playing. We brought those ratings way up, and that's why the NBA is making so much money. Some of these guys actually, truly believe they deserve $15 million a year. And the only reason they're getting it is Jordan.

Michael isn't going to be around forever on the court. It would be nice, but it's impossible. And the NBA is going to change when he leaves. You've got to remember something: People are so used to having him, so used to watching Michael every night, so used to getting ready for him coming to town. It's like when you go to your favorite restaurant.

COMPARING THE LEGENDS

	GP	RBS	AST	PTS	AVG.
Michael Jordan (1984-93, 1995-97)	848	5,361	4,729	26,920	31.7
Wilt Chamberlain (1959-73)	1,045	23,924	4,643	31,419	30.1
Elgin Baylor (1958-72)	846	11,463	3,650	23,149	27.4
Jerry West (1960-74)	932	5,376	6,238	25,192	27.0
Oscar Robertson (1960-74)	1,040	7,804	9,887	26,710	25.7
Kareem Abdul-Jabbar (1969-89)	1,560	17,440	5,660	38,387	24.6
Larry Bird (1979-92)	897	8,974	5,695	21,791	24.3
Julius Erving# (1971-87)	1,243	10,525	5,176	30,026	24.2
Magic Johnson (1979-91, 1995-96)	906	6,559	10,141	17,707	19.5

— combined NBA/ABA record

You want your favorite meal, and you want it cooked the same. When it changes, when there's a new chef, you say, "What? You're going crazy." It's the same with Michael. He's the chef. He's like fine wine, fine food. When you pull him from everybody, when he retires, everybody's going to miss him.

He elevated every home crowd, every home player. Everybody wants to touch him. He's going to be sorely missed, because we are waiting for the next guy to carry that torch. And I don't know who it's going to be.

What we're all going to remember about Michael, what he leaves behind, is not just going to be one thing. At least not in my mind. He is far bigger than just basketball. He brought such class. You know what it is? We're missing professionals now. He's such a pro's pro. He goes to practice, he does his job; he goes to the game, he does his job. He promotes the NBA. He'll go down as one of the game's greatest ambassadors, which is something you just can't overlook either. Here's why I love him: We're in Chicago working out at a sports club. Michael is just lifting weights. Some of the guys there are saying, "Wow, I wish I could play with Michael." I only had track shoes, but Michael had his shoes. So he goes out there on the court at this health club and plays with the guys. Do you know what that did for those dudes? They'll never forget that. He was just high-fiving and going around

dunking on guys. They loved it.

He touches people like nobody else. He's way, way bigger than the game, and he will always be up there. He doesn't have to play basketball. He's a super, super, superstar.

Sometimes when I lie in bed at night, I wish I could take off like Michael Jordan, just take off like him one time. I guess that's a dream. Believe me, I'm not the only one who ever wanted that same thing. See there, Michael Jordan can even have an impact on you when you're asleep.

For a lot of years, it's been a wonderful dream, I know that.

Earvin Magic Johnson, vice president and part owner of the Los Angeles Lakers, played with the Lakers for 13 years and led the team to five NBA championships (in 1980, '82, '85, '87 and '88). In those 13 years, which included 11 All-Star appearances for Johnson, L.A. played in the NBA Finals nine times and averaged 59 victories a season.

The Lakers' last Finals appearance with Johnson as a player came against Jordan and the Bulls in '91. The torch was passed as MJ and Co. defeated L.A. in five games to claim their first of three consecutive NBA championships.

Thomas Bonk, who interviewed Magic Johnson for this story, is a writer for the Los Angeles Times.

Cory, you are a bright and very talented young Man! Look to your heart and all of your Dream WILL come true!

Cory: It was a lot of fun having you part as the team this year. Your a pleasure to coach. Keep up the good work.

Larry Bird

Cory! You have an incredible amount of talent, not just in your good moves, but in the way you think! You have a wonderfully gentle nature - I hope you never lose it. Keep your head up! on the court, and all the way through life.

Coach Bob (Cermak?)